For Gabriel,
my 'boy eternal'

The Publishers would like to thank Barbara Godlee for her invaluable
research and encouragement.

© The Chicken House 2001

Illustrations © James Mayhew 2001

Storyboard by James Mayhew and Elinor Bagenal

First published in the United Kingdom in 2001 by
The Chicken House, 2 Palmer Street, Frome, Somerset, BA11 1DS

Designed by Lisa Sturley

Printed and bound in the U.A.E.

British Library Cataloguing in Publication data available.
Library of Congress Cataloging-in-Publication data available.

ISBN: 1 903434 12 2

WILLIAM SHAKESPEARE

TO SLEEP, PERCHANCE TO DREAM

A CHILD'S BOOK OF RHYMES

Illustrated by James Mayhew

Chicken The House

An Egmont joint venture

But, soft!
methinks I scent
the morning air.

Hamlet I v

Hark! hark! the lark at heaven's gate sings,
And Phoebus 'gins arise,
His steeds to water at those springs
On chalic'd flowers that lies;
And winking Mary-buds begin
To ope their golden eyes:
With every thing that pretty is,
My lady sweet, arise!

Cymbeline II III

It was a lover and his lass,
With a hey, and a ho, and a hey-nonny-no,
That o'er the green corn-field did pass,
In the spring-time, the only pretty ring-time,
When birds do sing, hey ding-a-ding, ding;
Sweet lovers love the spring.

As You Like It V III

All the world's a stage,
And all the men and women merely players.
They have their exits and their entrances,
And one man in his time plays many parts,
His acts being seven ages.

As You Like It II VII

We were, fair queen,
Two lads, that thought there was no more behind
But such a day tomorrow as today,
And to be boy eternal.

The Winter's Tale I II

And Liberty plucks Justice by the nose,
The baby beats the nurse, and quite athwart
Goes all decorum.

Measure for Measure I III

Come unto these yellow sands,
And then take hands;
Curtsied when you have, and kissed, –
The wild waves whist.

The Tempest I II

Since once I sat upon a promontory,
And heard a mermaid on a dolphin's back
Uttering such dulcet and harmonious breath,
That the rude sea grew civil at her song,
And certain stars shot madly from their spheres,
To hear the sea-maid's music.

A Midsummer Night's Dream II 1

How sweet the moonlight sleeps upon this bank!
Here will we sit, and let the sounds of music
Creep in our ears; soft stillness and the night
Become the touches of sweet harmony.

The Merchant of Venice V I

Philomel, with melody,
Sing in our sweet lullaby;
Lulla, lulla, lullaby; lulla, lulla, lullaby:
Never harm,
Nor spell, nor charm
Come our lovely lady nigh;
So, good night, with lullaby.

A Midsummer Night's Dream II II

I'll give thee fairies to attend on thee;
And they shall fetch thee jewels from the deep,
And sing, while thou on pressed flowers dost sleep.

A Midsummer Night's Dream III 1

We are such stuff as
dreams are made on,
and our little life is
rounded with a sleep.

*The Tempest IV*ɪ